A Day in the Life: Desert Animals

Meerkat

Anita Ganeri

www.raintreepublishers.co.uk
Visit our website to find out
more information about
Raintree books.

To order:
☎ Phone 0845 6044371
🖷 Fax +44 (0) 1865 312263
🖷 Email myorders@raintreepublishers.co.uk

Customers from outside the UK please telephone +44 1865 312262

Raintree is an imprint of Capstone Global Library Limited,
a company incorporated in England and Wales having
its registered office at 7 Pilgrim Street, London, EC4V 6LB
– Registered company number: 6695582

Text © Capstone Global Library Limited 2011
First published in hardback in 2011
The moral rights of the proprietor have been asserted.

Edited by Daniel Nunn, Rebecca Rissman, and Sian Smith
Designed by Richard Parker
Picture research by Elizabeth Alexander
Production by Victoria Fitzgerald
Originated by Capstone Global Library Ltd
Printed and bound in China by South China Printing
 Company Ltd

ISBN 978 1 406 21964 7 (hardback)
14 13 12 11 10
10 9 8 7 6 5 4 3 2 1

**British Library Cataloguing in Publication
Data**
Ganeri, Anita, 1961-
  Meerkat. -- (A day in the life. Desert animals)
  1. Meerkat--Juvenile literature.
  I. Title II. Series
  599.7'42-dc22

Acknowledgements

We would like to thank the following for permission to
reproduce photographs: Alamy pp. 13 (© WorldFoto/
Alamy), 21 (© AfriPics.com/Alamy); Carolyn Ireland p.
16; Corbis pp. 4, 14, 23 glossary groom, 23 glossary
mammal (© Paul A. Souders); FLPA pp. 7, 23 glossary
burrow (© Mark Newman), 8, 15 (© Vincent Grafhorst/
Minden Pictures), 17 (© Shem Compion); iStockphoto p.
5 (© Els van der Gun); Photolibrary pp. 9 (Peter Arnold
Images/Martin Harvey), 11 (Mark Newman/Superstock),
12 (David Macdonald/OSF), 20 (Gunter Ziesler/Peter
Arnold Images), 23 glossary poison (David Macdonald/
OSF); Shutterstock pp. 10, 23 glossary desert (© Karol
Kozlowski), 18, 19, 23 glossary predator (© EcoPrint), 22,
23 glossary claw (© Pyshnyy Maxim Vjacheslavovich), 23
glossary insect (© Anke van Wyk).

Front cover photograph of a suricate or meerkat (Suricata
suricatta) family, in the Kalahari Desert, South Africa
reproduced with permission of Shutterstock (© EcoPrint).

Back cover photograph of (left) a meerkat with pups
reproduced with permission of Corbis (© Paul Souders);
and (right) a suricate or meerkat (Suricata suricatta)
standing on guard, reproduced with permission of
Shutterstock (© EcoPrint).

We would like to thank Michael Bright for his assistance in
the preparation of this book.

Every effort has been made to contact copyright holders
of material reproduced in this book. Any omissions will
be rectified in subsequent printings if notice is given to the
publisher.

All the Internet addresses (URLs) given in this book were
valid at the time of going to press. However, due to the
dynamic nature of the Internet, some addresses may have
changed, or sites may have changed or ceased to exist
since publication. While the author and publisher regret
any inconvenience this may cause readers, no responsibility
for any such changes can be accepted by either the author
or the publisher.

Contents

Some words are shown in bold, **like this**.
You can find them in the glossary on page 23.

What is a meerkat?

A meerkat is a **mammal**.

All mammals have some hair on their bodies and feed their babies milk.

mongoose

Meerkats are about the size of large squirrels.

They belong to a group of mammals called mongooses.

Where do meerkats live?

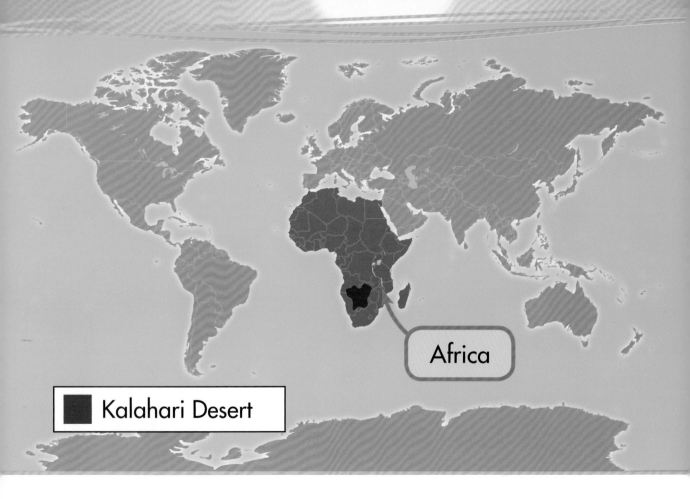

Africa

Kalahari Desert

Meerkats live in the Kalahari **Desert** in southern Africa.

It is hot and dry in the desert.

burrow

A lot of the desert is covered in sand.

The meerkats dig **burrows** in the sand or live in burrows dug by other animals.

What do meerkats look like?

Meerkats have long, thin bodies, covered in brown-grey fur.

They have large dark patches around their eyes.

Meerkats have long **claws** on their front feet for digging.

They use their tails for balancing when they are standing upright.

What do meerkats do in the day?

Meerkats come out of their **burrows** in the morning.

Then they lie in the sun to warm up.

Meerkats spend most of the day looking for food.

If it gets too hot, they shelter in their burrows or under a bush.

What do meerkats eat?

scorpion

Meerkats can eat scorpions without being harmed by their **poison**.

They also eat **desert insects**.

Meerkats can live without drinking water.

They get the water they need from eating desert plants and animals.

Do meerkats live in groups?

Meerkats live in large groups of up to 30 animals.

In the day, the meerkats **groom** each other and play together.

burrow

Each group lives in its own **burrow**.

The burrows have long tunnels with many entrance and exit holes.

Where are baby meerkats born?

Baby meerkats are born in the **burrows**.

In the day, other females in the group look after them while their mother hunts for food.

The babies go outside for the first time when they are four weeks old.

Their mother teaches them what kind of food to eat.

Does anything hunt meerkats?

jackal

While the meerkats are outside in the day, they have to look out for **predators**.

Jackals, eagles, and falcons like to hunt and eat meerkats.

The meerkats take it in turns to stand guard.

If the guard sees danger, it barks or whistles and the meerkats run back into their **burrows**.

What do meerkats do at night?

In the evening, it gets cold in the **desert**.

The meerkats stop feeding and go back into their **burrows** to sleep.

The meerkats only come out of their burrows next morning if it is warm and sunny.

If it is rainy or cloudy, they stay inside.

Meerkat body map

eye

ear

nose

fur

claws

foot

tail

Glossary

 **burrow** hole in the ground where a meerkat lives

 **claw** sharp, nail-like part of a meerkat's feet

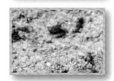 **desert** very dry place that is rocky, stony, or sandy

 **groom** clean each other's fur

 **insect** animal that has six legs, such as a grasshopper

 **mammal** animal that feeds its babies milk. All mammals have some hair or fur on their bodies.

 **poison** something that can cause illness or death

 **predator** animal that hunts other animals for food

Find out more

Books

Desert Animals (Focus on Habitats), Stephen Savage (Wayland, 2006)

Deserts (My World of Geography), Angela Royston (Heinemann Library, 2004)

24 Hours: Desert (Focus on Habitats), Elizabeth Haldane (Dorling Kindersley, 2006)

Websites

Watch a video on meerkats and find out all about them at:
kids.nationalgeographic.com/kids/animals/creaturefeature/meerkat

Learn more about meerkats at:
www.sandiegozoo.org/animalbytes/t-meerkat.html

Index